AF882365

What Our Readers Have Said...

Applicability

"These books are great tools that should be used as guidelines for our everyday supervisory practices. You need to take the time to do a short self-evaluation when reading them."

•

"The Pinpoint Training Series delivers information that could be used in a lot different areas."

•

"The things and problems we deal with everyday are discussed in these books."

Convenience

"I like this because I can take them with me to read at a convenient time. I feel the little time I have to spend in the office is best use on activities that directly relate to revenue opportunities. I like the short amount of time it takes to keep up with these."

•

"I prefer the self-study approach; it fits in with my schedule."

•

"I like the fact that the format allows the books to be reviewed as time permits. All work has been conducted on personal, evening/weekend time."

•

"Easy to use... if you put the time into it."

Challenge

"My thought is that the real value of these books comes into effect when doing the action plans."

•

"I like the fact that the format allows assignments to be reviewed as time permits."

Clarity

"Short and sweet. These books are easy to comprehend."

•

"Easy to use, understand, and reference if needed."

Relevance

"I have enjoyed reading these books. They are relevant to today's work environment and the ongoing change in the way we manage our workforce."

•

"I believe the contents of the Pinpoint series are excellent. It causes one to reflect on the daily dynamics in working with oneself as well as with management and peers."

Roles & Responsibilities of Delegation

Pinpoint Leadership Skill Development Training Series

TIMOTHY F. BEDNARZ

MAJORIUM
BUSINESS PRESS

Pinpoint Leadership Skill Development Training Series
"Roles & Responsibilities of Delegation"
Timothy F. Bednarz

Graphic design: Monika Pawlak

Majorium Business Press
2025 Main Street
Stevens Point, WI 54481
715.342.1018 • 800.654.4935

ISBN 978-1-62101-044-9

Printed in the United States of America

Introduction

The Pinpoint Leadership Skill Development Training Series is designed for targeted training and education regarding increased improvement in a specific skill or competency.

Each book within this series is designed to be easy to use, understand and apply to your job. It can be used as a basis for training individuals, as a discussion guide or as a personal training tool.

Each chapter within this book discusses a specific concept. When you have completed all eight chapters you should have a 360° perspective of the topic.

Additionally, each chapter is divided into specific sections:

- The first section provides you with an overview of the topic
- The Implications section discusses why the concept is important, and why it is important to learn and apply.
- The Strategies, Tips & Techniques to Apply section teaches how to use and apply the particular concept to your work.
- The Points to Ponder section gives you something to think about or to be discussed with a group setting. These are questions not meant to be immediately answered, but to be pondered over time.
- The Training Activity section provides you with the tools to transfer what you have learned to your job. It is designed to help create an action plan to effectively apply the concept.

Each of the topics in this series is time-tested and proven in the marketplace. They have been used by thousands of employees as training tools. Many of the users have commented that what made these books valuable, was the ability to refer to them when a problem surfaced. They indicated that they remembered reading about the exact problem. They referred back to these books and found an appropriate solution.

You will find them equally valuable as a resource in your professional development library.

Table of Contents

LEARNING OBJECTIVES:

- The role of delegation in their success as a leader.
- To define the roles and responsibilities of delegation.
- To assign and educate subordinates about delegated duties.
- To effectively monitor and evaluate delegation performance.

1

Why Delegation Is an Essential Skill

When many leaders are asked, „Do you delegate as much as you should?" the response often is, "Probably not. I can't take the time to train someone, let alone trust them to complete assignments I am personally responsible for." Many don't fully realize why they should delegate.

Leaders understand the importance of effectively utilizing every resource they have at their disposal. This includes the people they direct and lead.

IMPLICATIONS – WHAT THIS MEANS TO YOU

Leaders must appreciate the power delegation brings to their individual units as well as to the organization as a whole. When they start to actively delegate, three things begin to take place that positively transform the workplace and personal performance.

STRATEGIES, TIPS & TECHNIQUES TO APPLY

When leaders as effective leaders delegate, their employees begin to increase their knowledge, which better equips them to make decisions, solve problems and generate more productive end results. These enhancements work to improve overall workplace and organizational performance. This is why delegation is so powerful: utilizing their employee's abilities and talents as a resource, leaders move toward their goals at a much faster pace. Understanding how and why these three elements positively affect personal performance is helpful in creating the desire to delegate.

Increasing in Knowledge

Increasing an employee's knowledge builds an in-depth understanding of information. When employees are delegated a task or assignment and complete it effectively, they can transfer this knowledge to other new situations. This builds a broader base of knowledge, which renders new assignments easier to complete.

Past experiences make up a large majority of anyone's knowledge base. All active responses are based upon previous positive or negative events. When leaders delegate effectively, they help build positive experiences for their employees, which works to motivate them to achieve at higher levels.

Increasing an employee's experience level helps them create a better base on which to judge situations and circumstances. When a leader delegates, the assignment or task directly alters how the employee perceives the realities they encounter. They can better relate to the leader who carries the majority of responsibility and accountability. They also connect more closely with coworkers because a sense of loyalty is built into the total delegated experience.

Problem Solving

Effective and ongoing delegation enhances employees' problem solving abilities. Leaders use the delegation of tasks and assignments to coach their people in how to sift facts from misinformation. This gives them a real tool that provides them with shortcuts to solving a problem or addressing a major concern faster and more effectively. It also aids in helping employees establish their own goals and priorities. In this way, they can easily determine which direction is best to take and why. In delegated tasks and assignments, leaders need to emphasize that looking at problems from various perspectives helps uncover the root causes of problems rather than their symptoms.

Crafting Unique Solutions

One main reason delegation is so powerful is because it improves effective decision making skills.

Leaders understand how formational decision making is in each of their employee's personal and professional lives. By delegating assignments and tasks, leaders help improve decision making skills by introducing previously unconsidered perspectives of how to approach assignments. They also give suggestions and offer shortcuts so that employees can immediately arrive at productive determinations and feel successful. Good leaders are great role models for proper decision making.

Delegation is an excellent way to teach employees how to prioritize their time and associated responsibilities. Prioritizing is indispensable to effective problem solving, which, when mastered, cuts back on frustration and enables employees to think more clearly and arrive at better solutions.

When a leader delegates, their employees gain a better understanding of what does and does not work in certain situations. They allow employees to use trial and error to accomplish their assignments or tasks, which works to decrease the time and risks associated with solving future problems.

POINTS TO PONDER — SOMETHING TO THINK ABOUT

1. Do you find yourself delegating less often than you should? Why?
2. Why in terms of your own leadership position do you feel delegation is important?

TRAINING ACTIVITY — APPLICATION & ACTION PLAN

List several tasks or assignments that can be just as easily accomplished by someone who normally doesn't volunteer.

1. Delegate the task.
2. Motivate and personally work with the individual as they accomplish their delegated assignment.
3. Stress the benefits of why delegating is personally important to them and what benefits they will receive because of it.
4. Observe to see whether their personal and professional attitude changes.

2

Leaders Lead in the Delegation of Assignments and Tasks

Leaders assume many responsibilities, which taken together ultimately define their complete role. Delegating effectively is one such responsibility.

IMPLICATIONS — WHAT THIS MEANS TO YOU

Defining the role of leadership from a delegation standpoint is essential to leaders because they must always be focused in terms of creating effective results and utilizing their resources to the fullest. Leaders need to continually address the question, "Do I delegate effectively and often enough to best accomplish my goals?"

It is not enough to simply assign tasks to individual employees. Leaders take great care to identify the best candidates for the delegation of assignments, get personally involved in setting appropriate and consistent standards, and follow up to ensure they are successfully completed. These actions foster employee growth, which ultimately guarantees that more challenging assignments can be delegated in the future. Leaders are then able to grow their organization and increase results through mutual efforts.

STRATEGIES, TIPS & TECHNIQUES TO APPLY

Leaders must analyze the following three areas carefully if they wish to move themselves, their employees and their organization forward. In order to use the delegation of employees as a valuable resource, leaders set and maintain high standards. They target employees for specific tasks and assignments, encouraging them to become more personally involved in their work by using their abilities and talents to the fullest. They understand that all these efforts without their own personal involvement diminishes the overall positive results they wish to obtain.

Solid and appropriate standards help move employees consistently through the completion of each task in relation to overall assignments. Understanding how to do this effectively, includes:

Setting and Maintaining High Standards

Many leaders have difficulty defining appropriate standards when it comes to delegating. If standards are set too high, tasks and assignments will seldom, if ever, be achieved. If standards are set too low, success will be guaranteed, and employees will feel good about their accomplishments, but their use as a valuable resource is greatly diminished.

Standards must be consistent and appropriate for the tasks and assignments delegated. Establishing solid standards ensures that goals and assignments are attained on a timely basis and are accomplished in ways that move the leader and organization forward. Setting and applying standards cannot be divorced from the delegation process. Each employee must be aware of the expectations specific standards place on him or her. In order for delegation to be effective, each employee must be agreeable to the standards set and strive to meet them to the best of their ability.

Matching Employees to Specific Tasks and Assignments

It is important not to just match skills, abilities and personal motivation, but to factor in the employee's degree of perseverance, their personal work style and coping skills.

Leaders take careful consideration in weighing other factors involved in completing delegated assignments, including time, productivity and endurance. They match these factors to the responsibilities delegated.

Each employee's strengths and weaknesses are analyzed and weighed. The strengths are targeted and linked to whomever a leader feels can best accomplish the delegated assignment effectively, in a given time frame and with minimal support.

Personal Involvement in Delegated Assignments

In order to complete assignments and tasks, leaders use motivational factors to move each employee forward in their progress. Taking a proactive stance to be there when a problem or question arises sustains momentum and ensures that each assignment is completed successfully.

Active support for each employee and their assignment is crucial. Leaders help in various ways to make sure assignments are carried out step-by-step. They help employees to be thorough and focused by discussing various ways to increase their performance and make assignments and tasks less complicated and easier to complete.

Personal involvement in delegated assignments includes helping employees set their own goals and objectives to attain the desired outcome. When employees are given an active role in detailing their personal responsibilities, assignments and tasks become personalized. This personalization fosters an ownership in the assignment itself and in successfully attaining desired outcomes.

POINTS TO PONDER — SOMETHING TO THINK ABOUT

1. Do you currently set standards for delegated tasks or assignments?
2. What methods do you use to match employees to specific assignments and tasks? Are the results you generally obtain positive?

TRAINING ACTIVITY – APPLICATION & ACTION PLAN

Select one major goal you wish to accomplish.

1. Think of one specific assignment that can be delegated to further its attainment.
2. Target various employees as candidates and select the one you feel to be the best match.
3. Together with the employee, detail the standards and clearly define their responsibilities. Help him or her personally define the goals and objectives needed to complete the assignment or task.
4. Monitor the employee's progress by staying actively involved in their assignment.

3

Selecting the Right Employees for Delegation

A leader has multiple responsibilities to fulfill in order to be effective in the skillful application of delegation. Evaluating and selecting the most capable candidate is vital to the overall success of assignments and tasks.

IMPLICATIONS — WHAT THIS MEANS TO YOU

Proper delegation and defining of an employee's role are vital if the individual is to become a valuable and reliable resource. Effective evaluation of employees becomes a key issue. It is essential that leaders delegate tasks and assignments carefully with the employee's capabilities in mind. Effective delegation ensures that the right candidates are selected based upon their individual ability and desire to perform the assignment in an effective and timely manner.

Leaders understand that their role is to aid in their employee's growth by stretching their capabilities. They also understand that indiscriminate delegation undermines collective efforts and drains time and resources.

STRATEGIES, TIPS & TECHNIQUES TO APPLY

Leaders take great care when selecting a delegation candidate. Understanding that choosing the wrong candidates undermines their desire to delegate future assignments, leaders make it a point to personally know each individual employee and understand their motivation, work styles, personalities, desires, abilities, strengths and weaknesses. They understand the power the proper candidate brings to the workplace. He or she can increase overall productivity and help leaders attain set goals while reducing the time it takes to reach them. Selecting a proper delegation candidate hinges upon three major factors:

Desire to Accept Responsibility

Employees are good delegation candidates when they openly ask questions that search out knowledge regarding the department or organization and their role in it. This stance shows a desire to accept more responsibility and be a more active participant in shaping outcomes.

A good potential delegation candidate searches for ways to increase their knowledge base and be educated in new skills and concepts. When employees ask questions as to how to better themselves personally and professionally, they immediately should be targeted as a possible candidate for taking on more responsibility.

Leaders look for employees who have a personal need to feel successful. These individuals generally offer to lend a hand when their peers need assistance. They work well with others to complete tasks or assignments and want to be recognized as a helpful, valuable member of the organization. A service attitude is a good indicator that an employee will likely be a good candidate for cooperating successfully, taking on more responsibility, and fulfilling their role.

Motivation and Determination

Leaders recognize that the best delegation candidates display high levels of motivation. These people can complete delegated tasks and assignments with a minimum amount of prodding and assistance. They look for the positive side of things and generally accept and accomplish their tasks and assignments with high levels of enthusiasm.

Good delegation candidates stay on course in their work, looking for ways to overcome obstacles hindering their performance. They take their jobs seriously and work each individual task to its timely completion. This displays a focus of direction that is necessary for accomplishing tasks and assignments carefully, efficiently and effectively.

When it comes to a possible delegation candidate, leaders look for employees that don't get sidetracked and don't allow interferences to hinder their output. They are polite but show little interest when others wish to waste their time in trivial matters and general conversation. This seriousness in tending to their tasks displays a high level of determination.

Willingness to Improve

Track records can be extremely helpful when selecting a good delegation candidate. Past performance provides an indicator of how a potential candidate will likely function, and at what level, in newly assigned responsibilities. Prior work also indicates a rate of completion of past tasks and assignments, which also helps determine how a possible candidate will perform.

Leaders realize that not all candidates openly display the characteristics that define a good choice. Some employees have the desire to improve their performance but are assigned to jobs that offer them little room to advance or voice their desire to improve. Leaders find it helpful to candidly ask them how they feel about accepting more responsibility and increasing their duties and performance.

Good delegation candidates are always accepting of their tasks, assignments and responsibilities. They never turn down a chance to try something new just to see if they are able to accomplish it. The desire to be challenged indicates a willingness to improve one's circumstances, talents and abilities.

POINTS TO PONDER — SOMETHING TO THINK ABOUT

1. What characteristics are most important when choosing a good delegation candidate?
2. What methods have you used to select a delegation candidate in the past? Were your efforts to match the best employee to the right assignment successful? Why or why not?

TRAINING ACTIVITY — APPLICATION & ACTION PLAN

Create a list of all the factors detailed in the lesson that determine a successful delegation candidate.

1. Make several copies to use as you search for a delegation candidate.
2. Write an individual's name on the top of each copy as you begin to target each employee that may be a good candidate.
3. Use this as a check off list when searching for an ideal employee to delegate an assignment or task to.
4. Select the candidate who displays the highest number of positive factors.

4

Screening Delegates Through Assessment

Delegating responsibilities effectively is a key factor in a leader's successful achievement of their vision, direction and goals.

Dissecting total projects and verbally assessing each employee candidate is key to delegating effectively. Once accomplished, leaders are able to define and assign projects, assignments, tasks and responsibilities for the greatest degree of success.

IMPLICATIONS – WHAT THIS MEANS TO YOU

For leaders to both meet their own expectations and exceed the goals set by upper management, they must implement strategies to define and delegate specific responsibilities for maximum results.

Understanding and effectively applying an appropriate screening and assessment method is essential in this process. It is best accomplished through a leader's personal analysis of specific tasks and each candidate's readiness to perform them, as well as by addressing the personal motivational factors that will help carry the employee selected through individual assignment phases.

Even when leaders get to the point where they deem an employee an ideal candidate for a delegated task, there are several other issues to be considered. Addressing these issues assures that delegated tasks and assignments will be performed effectively and efficiently. Unless initial time is taken to carefully assess employees' capabilities, motivation and attitude, the leader may need to devote more subsequent time and energy to monitoring their progress.

STRATEGIES, TIPS & TECHNIQUES TO APPLY

Performing a comprehensive assessment of each candidate for delegation is essential for a successful selection process. Leaders look for candidates that measure up to their expectations and to the responsibilities they will be assigned. They carefully address and analyze specific concerns within three assessment categories before a proper candidate is finally selected for any given assignment.

Task

The leader's first step in the delegation screening assessment process is to specify the tasks or assignments he or she wishes to delegate. This is accomplished by analyzing the overall project for delegation. It is then broken down into smaller segments while the exact number of individuals needed is verified by the predetermined workloads.

As many delegated projects are complex in nature, a task assessment allows leaders to focus on detailing all the various assignments needed to complete the total project. Each one is viewed and addressed as a separate goal. As a goal, specific objectives to achieve it must be addressed and detailed. Once leaders define the whole project from the perspective of individual assignments and related goals, they begin to assess the employee's readiness to complete the responsibilities accordingly.

A complete, detailed listing of each individual task or assignment is prepared before meeting with selected candidates. The basis for the screening analysis, this listing is used to determine each candidate's desire and ability to successfully complete a delegated assignment and their willingness to accept the various responsibilities attached to it.

Responsibility Readiness

Leaders find it is helpful to carefully assess both the responsibility readiness and the ability level of a candidate. Such an assessment includes asking each selected candidate several questions in the areas of experience, training, understanding and clarity. Leaders carefully use the questions below and analyze the responses in these four categories. They take notes as a written reference tool that aids in determining their final choice for the assignment.

Experience

- Have you performed a task exactly like or similar to this assignment?
- Will you tell me how you did it?
- How long did it take?
- What steps did you take to accomplish the assignment?
- How long ago was the task assignment?
- Can you tell me how this current task is similar or relates to your previous task?

Training

- Do you have any special training or education that will help accomplish this assignment?
- Have you had any hands-on training that could apply to accomplishing this assignment?

Understanding

- How would you approach this assignment?
- Can you walk me through an orderly arrangement of the steps you would take?
- Describe the process or processes you would use in each step.
- What part of the assignment do you feel is most important? Why?

Clarity

- Do you understand this assignment will be your total responsibility?
- Do you feel you can handle this responsibility in a given time frame of (insert your expectation)?

Motivational Assessment

Leaders realize that the responsibility readiness and ability discussion weighs heavily upon the motivational assessment and is a key indicator of whether an employee will accept or resist the delegated portion of a project. An effective motivational assessment includes listening carefully to what is and is not being said in each interviewed employee's answers to the following questions:

Confidence

- How do you feel about taking on this assignment?
- Do you have any questions about the assignment that weren't answered up to now?
- Do you have any concerns about taking on the assignment?

Security

- Do you feel comfortable moving ahead with this assignment?
- What kind of help may you want or need?
- Do you understand that you can come to me anytime you need assistance?

Incentive

- Can you see any personal benefits attached to taking on this responsibility?
- Are they an incentive to help complete the assignment successfully?
- Can you think of how this assignment will help you in the future?

Desire

- Do you want to take on this delegated assignment?
- Are you willing to do the task(s) to the best of your ability?

POINTS TO PONDER – SOMETHING TO THINK ABOUT

1. Have you previously used an assessment tool for screening delegates for your assignments?
2. Have you delegated whole projects in the past or individual portions of a project? Why?

TRAINING ACTIVITY – APPLICATION & ACTION PLAN

Take one project you feel can be delegated effectively.

1. Select several potential candidates.
2. Apply the assessment in the three categories of Tasks, Responsibility and Ability Readiness and Motivation.
3. Select the best overall candidates and assign specific tasks for each to accomplish in a given time frame.
4. Monitor the assignments closely, offering assistance whenever needed.

5

Educating Employees

Leaders teach employees how to perform their delegated assignments and tasks in order to assure their timely and accurate completion. An effective method of educating employees both ensures complete understanding of assignments and addresses productive ways to complete them successfully.

IMPLICATIONS — WHAT THIS MEANS TO YOU

When tasks are delegated, many leaders become frustrated by the inability of employees to complete assignments in a timely and competent manner. Leaders often feel completing assignments by themselves is easier and faster. This becomes an excuse and a barrier to delegating altogether. It also hampers the leader's ability to grow and increase their productivity.

Leaders understand that when they begin to delegate tasks and assignments, time and patience are needed to educate their employees to perform competently.

Leaders regularly delegate assignments, but continue to see employees fall short of assignment completion and the expectations set for them. This is often the result of assignments or tasks being misunderstood, ignored, forgotten or viewed as overwhelming. These negative outcomes are generally attributed to improper or ineffective employee education.

Leaders know that in order to increase productivity and results, the first step is to properly educate their employees in how they want the task and assignment carried out and how specifically to do it. Employees must also be made aware of set time frames for accomplishing the work and the desired results the leader expects.

While employees may stumble initially, leaders understand that their proficiency will increase greatly with time and experience.

STRATEGIES, TIPS & TECHNIQUES TO APPLY

Use of the following six-step instructional method is a top priority for leaders because it eliminates unsuccessful assignment implementation and completion.

Review the Assignment

In order to effectively educate employees, leaders begin by previewing the overall assignment, task or responsibility. They look at all the components necessary to complete it effectively in a timely fashion and review their personal expectations in regard to it. Developing notes and reference points to use when meeting with individuals to be assigned is essential.

Explain Clearly and Carefully

One main responsibility in educating employees is to make instructions as clear and precise as possible. Leaders know that explaining clearly is a twofold process. They need to present their information in a way that is logical and free of confusion or ambiguity. The other side of clarity is how an employee perceives, interprets and responds to the instructions.

Leaders make it a point to use vocabulary that is on the employee's level of understanding. Specific examples are used that relate directly to the tasks and expectations within the given assignment. Leaders carefully organize and sequence the components of each task to be assigned. They eliminate irrelevant or unrelated information and are logical and realistic in their expectations and requirements.

Apply 'Think Time'

It is vital to explain in detail the work that needs to be done. Leaders need to both offer ideas or suggestions as to how best accomplish it and build in "think time" for employees to ponder and absorb what is being said. These are pauses inserted between major points of discussion, and include various essential components related to the task or the employee's questions regarding the assignment.

There is a time difference between hearing and comprehending. People talk much faster than one can actually listen. This is why leaders make it a point to explain small portions of an overall assignment within a given time frame, affording the necessary space for employees to think through the instructions and various responsibilities that apply to all aspects of their assignment. Additional time is allowed to formulate questions and concerns so employees feel thoroughly prepared.

Assign Reference Materials and Individual Resource People

There may be times throughout the course of an assignment when an employee needs to use outside resources. Leaders cover these contingencies in their instructions.

Employees should be given the names of two or more people that can help them in problem situations. Reference materials should also be offered with detailed explanations of how they can be used and for what types of situations. Discussions and illustrations on how and where to find solutions to problems pertaining to their assignments need to be included in the instructional process.

Repeat and Readdress Directions and Specific Points

As total understanding is key to task achievement, leaders consistently repeat and readdress major points, issues and detailed components of assignments. This repetition focuses the employee's attention on what is being said. Repeating and readdressing issues also helps leaders avoid inserting last-minute changes in their assignments and/or instructions. It is also a good way to survey the understanding levels of an employee. Leaders find many employees are ready to begin their assignments immediately after one good instructional period. Many will need little or no intervention and prodding afterward.

Self-Test for Assignment Understanding

Leaders encourage employees to test themselves in instructional areas that are not clear to them. The process includes being able to identify and openly state the main idea of the various components, steps, actions and responsibilities in their assignments. They should be able to recall exact directives of each separate phase of their assignment. Employees should be able to verbally detail what they need to do, when it needs to be done, and how best to accomplish it.

Ideas, concepts, methods or areas that remain unclear need to be revisited. Instructions should be given again in a learning style best suited to achieving total understanding. Leaders find that self-testing works effectively at the end of an instructional period to review and solidify the various details and processes within the given assignments.

POINTS TO PONDER — SOMETHING TO THINK ABOUT

1. Do you currently set aside a given amount of time as an instructional period for delegated assignments?
2. Have you previously used any of the above instructional methods when delegating assignments?

TRAINING ACTIVITY — APPLICATION & ACTION PLAN

Select one employee for a delegated assignment. Develop an instructional plan using the following steps:

1. Review the assignment or task carefully before meeting with the employee.
2. Explain the assignment clearly and carefully.

3. Incorporate “Think Time” into the instructional period.
4. Assign reference materials and individual resource people if needed.
5. Repeat and readdress your directions and specific points.
6. Allow the employee to self-test for assignment understanding.

6

Implementing Delegation

Proper delegation implementation procedures are vital to leadership success. In order to accomplish effective delegation there must be a focus and purpose that guarantees its success. The process a leader uses determines the failure or success of delegating.

IMPLICATIONS — WHAT THIS MEANS TO YOU

Many leaders think they effectively delegate by assigning tasks they consider to be unessential or unimportant. Employees take this personally. They believe these leaders are working to undermine their potential and ability.

Leaders need to review given assignments from various perspectives. This allows them to be concise and meaningful. Without developing clarity in delegated assignments, they are guaranteed to fall short of expectations.

Leaders need to develop a step-by-step implementation procedure to make the delegation process flow smoothly. Effective delegation is one of the most powerful tools they have to move their organization and themselves forward. Leaders need to make sure that the process they use is proactive and easily monitored to bring about the best results.

STRATEGIES, TIPS & TECHNIQUES TO APPLY

A seven-step process ensures one's delegation implementation is complete, effective and successful. Each step builds upon the other. For attaining the best results, they should be followed in the sequence below.

Determine Tasks and Responsibilities

Tasks and responsibilities must fit into the big picture of how they work to attain a leader's overall goals and objectives. Selecting each assignment, task and responsibility in a prioritized sequence allows them to be assigned accordingly.

Some leaders believe they are continually delegating effectively. In fact, many only assign tasks that are of a low priority, or unessential. Each delegated activity must have a definite purpose. It must also be linked to an objective that accomplishes individual goals.

Determine the Scope of Responsibilities

The manner in which the scope of responsibilities is conveyed to the employee determines how effective the delegated assignment becomes. Many leaders make a list, whether in writing or verbally, of "by's" such as, "By working in this department you are expected to make..." or, "By producing 20% more you will be able to..." These "by's" tend to undermine employee motivation.

Instead, leaders define the scope of delegated responsibilities by addressing the assignment clearly and concisely. They describe exactly what has to be accomplished and when it needs to be completed. They further detail suggestions as to how the assignment can best be accomplished. They define the areas where the employee will be expected to increase productivity, why they are expected to do it, and why their assignment is vital to the both unit's and the leader's success.

Review Assignments

Part of a leader's delegation responsibility includes reviewing given assignments from various perspectives. Reviewing assignments allows them to be concise and meaningful. In order to accomplish this effectively, leaders review and address assignments by asking themselves several questions.

- "Is this assignment concise and as simple as I can make it?"
- "Is this particular assignment targeted to my selected employee?"
- "What is the best way to deliver the assignment and the responsibilities attached to it?"
- "Does the assignment identify why it is necessary?"
- "How can I make a strong case for its purpose?"
- "How will I identify the actions I wish this particular employee to take?"
- "How should I address the more difficult or sensitive aspects of its completion?"
- "Does this assignment reinforce the company's shared values?"

Once these questions are formulated with the appropriate responses, delegated assignments become completely and thoroughly reviewed.

Put the Employee at Ease

When initially meeting with employees, leaders need to make sure they are put at ease. Increasing their comfort level develops a better understanding and acceptance of the information provided. Good leaders often insert bits of humor to lighten the implementation process. They reflect upon the feelings of the other person and respond to them to show empathy and understanding. This works to build a strong relationship with the employee from the start of the delegation process.

Effectiveness demands that leaders spend no more than two minutes in general conversation before moving forward to relevant topic details and issues.

Present the Assignment

Leaders find the TSIQ approach very helpful in presenting information when implementing the delegating process. Comprised of Telling, Showing, Illustrating and Questioning, the TSIQ approach supplies the knowledge needed for the conditions, skills, details and expectations of the delegated assignment.

Information within presentations needs to be administered slowly, clearly, completely and patiently. Leaders should address one point at a time so that errors of thought and miscommunication can be immediately clarified. Checking, questioning and repeating necessary information once it has been initially presented works to eliminate the need for backtracking and clears up misinterpretations and misunderstandings. Leaders should continue the presentation until they can ascertain what the employee knows.

Develop and Agree Upon a Completion Plan and Specific Evaluation Criteria to Monitor Performance

Delegated assignments are ineffective unless there is mutual agreement on deadlines. The criteria that define the steps and priorities needed to complete assignments must be appropriate. Completion plans are addressed after the reviewing stage. Employees have input into the plan's evaluation process. Time frames for specific assignment steps are determined. Specific assignment aspects and details needing consistent evaluation are identified. This information must be put into a prioritized, written format and used at designated periods throughout various assignment phases. Leaders need to understand the importance of including coaching guidelines as part of their planning and monitoring criteria.

Coach, Advise and Guide

Implementing delegated assignments must include techniques that coach and guide employees in completing their assignments effectively and timely. Guiding is not directing, but means being there for an employee when problems or concerns surface, and helping each one work through them.

Coaching is used to reinforce concepts and techniques to accomplish various aspects of an assignment. Because of this, leaders must allow employees to help set their own goals and priorities. They need to allow employees to use their own personal work styles to accomplish specific tasks and projects.

POINTS TO PONDER — SOMETHING TO THINK ABOUT

1. When delegating assignments, how often do you conduct a thorough review of them?
2. Do you currently define delegated assignments in terms of a definite purpose directly linked to your corporate objectives?

TRAINING ACTIVITY — APPLICATION & ACTION PLAN

Select two or more assignments to delegate. Write out each one separately and outline the necessary information needed to complete the following steps:

1. Determine what specific tasks are needed to complete each assignment. Define the integrated and associated responsibilities for each of the specific tasks that lead to its completion.
2. Determine the scope of responsibilities attached to specific tasks and the overall assignment.
3. Review each overall assignment, while addressing the questions included in this lesson.
4. Together with each delegated employee, agree upon a completion plan that defines tasks, responsibilities, time frames, and evaluation criteria that will be used to monitor their performance.

7

Monitoring and Coaching Performance

Effective leaders manage by keeping their finger on the pulse of their employees' key activities. When tasks and assignments are delegated, leaders must take the time to review each employee's progress against goals to determine what, if any, additional training and coaching is needed to successfully complete the assignment or to enhance his or her skills.

IMPLICATIONS — WHAT THIS MEANS TO YOU

There is a twofold purpose of an assignment performance review. Leaders are receiving a progress report on the delegated task or assignment. They are allowing the employee to provide details and input on what has happened to date, and the results. The employee is also providing feedback on any problems, issues and concerns that may have surfaced. This allows the leader to provide insights and to suggest possible courses of action, if needed.

The second aspect of an assignment performance review is to assess professional employee growth and skill development. Properly performed, an assignment performance review allows leaders to guide and direct the professional development of their employees. This is the most important aspect of the review.

The purpose of delegation is not only to assign tasks and assignments, but to build and polish an employee's skills and capabilities. Only when this happens can leaders know with confidence that tasks and assignments can be successfully delegated, and overall performance and results increased.

STRATEGIES, TIPS & TECHNIQUES TO APPLY

When leaders monitor an employee's performance, they are performing a mixture of a work and planning review with a developmental planning review.

A work and planning review directs and controls the employee's performance in the traditional management sense, while a developmental planning review is designed to assist the employee in improving his or her personal skills. When reviewing the progress of a delegated assignment or task, the leader is doing both.

During an assignment performance review, the leader is reviewing the actual progress toward specific goals of the employee while also assessing his or her knowledge, attitude and on-the-job skills. During the review, leaders are not controlling and directing but seeking balanced input from the employee. In this manner, problems, issues and concerns are discussed while the leader probes with questions to identify the degree to which the employee has worked to resolve them. Leaders provide their insight or advice only after employees have given a full report of their progress, the problems and issues that have arisen, and the various alternatives they have tried.

Throughout performance assessments, leaders need to build trust and rapport with their employees to develop deeper levels of loyalty. There are several things leaders need to avoid so the relationship with their employee is not undermined during these reviews. These include:

Unwarranted Criticism

Leaders should base their judgments and criticisms on facts, not supposition. They must avoid making unwarranted negative comments or judgments about the employee's performance, attitude and decisions.

Analyzing the Employee's Motivation

Leaders should avoid playing the role of an "amateur psychiatrist" by not analyzing an employee's motives or behaviors.

Controlling and Directing

Leaders should avoid giving a detailed solution to existing problems without asking employees for their input.

Threatening and Coercion

Since leaders are using delegation to develop employee skills, they should avoid at all costs any attempts to coerce and force an employee to do things their way. They should avoid threatening employees with intimidating and negative consequences.

Questioning

Leaders should avoid second-guessing their employees with questions about every idea, decision, recommendation or suggestion. The purpose of the performance review is to analyze performance regarding a delegated task and to assess how employee skills have improved.

Once the initial phase of the review has been performed and the assignment thoroughly discussed, the leader and employee should agree upon an action plan for the remaining portions of the project. The leader should include any plans for self-improvement and growth the employee may require, which may include additional training or coaching in specific skill areas.

Whatever the actual plans, leaders should make sure they are realistic, attainable, measurable and on a scheduled timeline. Both the leader and the employee should know what will be done and how, and detailed milestones that the employee needs to achieve must be set.

POINTS TO PONDER — SOMETHING TO THINK ABOUT

1. What is your personal style of reviewing the tasks and assignments delegated to employees?
2. How do you build trust, rapport and loyalty in your employees?

TRAINING ACTIVITY — APPLICATION & ACTION PLAN

Develop an assignment performance review for your employees.

1. Compare the employee's outputs and activities against the agreed upon goals and standards.
2. Determine areas where the employee is experiencing problems.
3. Identify all approaches to solving the problem that the employee has used.
4. Determine the insights and solutions you can offer to the employee.
5. Identify the areas where the employee needs to improve.
6. Identify the facts to support your evaluation.
7. Identify the specific improvements you wish to see in the employee.
8. Determine professional development activities or coaching that can be offered to the employee.
9. Determine scheduled follow-ups.

8

Assigning Workgroup Roles Is an Effective Part of Delegation

Delegation is more than just assigning tasks and obligations from an individual standpoint. At times it may be necessary to bring groups of individuals together to work collaboratively toward completing total projects. This includes assigning roles within these workgroups. Roles are used to create effective project outcomes by reducing risks and improving decision making abilities, and thus assuring higher productivity and effective solutions.

IMPLICATIONS – WHAT THIS MEANS TO YOU

Roles acknowledge there is an interaction among people. Effective leaders know that results are produced through their employees. Delegating single tasks will not always move the organizational unit forward. If optimum performance is to be realized, leaders have to blend their employees into effective workgroups that have the ability to maximize their performance and sustain increased results over time.

A leader's most essential resource in maximizing performance and improving productivity, efficiency and profitability is fully using their employees' abilities. Leaders have two options: employees can simply perform the assigned tasks detailed within their individual job descriptions, or leaders can begin to maximize their people's potential by delegating projects to workgroups.

In many company settings, employees work as groups, not necessarily as self-functioning teams. Leaders educate employees to work together using varied roles that guide and direct their activities. These roles are often assigned under a leader's supervision, enabling them to perform at much higher levels.

Collaboration of workgroups focuses on the accomplishment of projects comprised of common goals and objectives. By blending employees into groups, more can be accomplished since projects utilize combined talents, skills, capabilities and perspectives.

Assigning specific workgroup roles assures that employees are empowered to accept more responsibility, contribute their ideas, and offer and accept feedback. This creates an atmosphere of accountability.

STRATEGIES, TIPS & TECHNIQUES TO APPLY

Individual employees possess different levels of abilities and capabilities. Successful delegation involves viewing and analyzing the overall goals of a group project. Once completed, leaders blend their employees to highlight their unified strengths while minimizing their weaknesses. Each member needs to complement the other members within the group. This creates a strong working unit and makes it easier to assign tasks, objectives and roles that contribute to the project's success.

Each individual employee must be assigned a role within the group that needs to be fulfilled if the group as a whole is to be successful. When applying role assignments, it is easier to assign tasks and objectives that contribute to the group's success.

Defining Roles

There is a difference between assigning roles and delegating tasks. Once assigned to a given project, it is important to determine which group member is best suited to perform specific role aspects within project assignments. Individual group members are selected for each role. As projects and assignments change, so can role assignments. Because of their skills, training or ability, certain individuals are better suited to fulfill specific roles for different projects. A leader may desire to switch roles to develop an individual employee's competency and comfort level in fulfilling various responsibilities.

The basic workgroup roles assigned typically include: Group Leader, Coordinator, Communicator, Monitor and Evaluator.

The group leader will be the individual assigned the role of leading the group during a specific assignment. In this role, he or she will run all group meetings and be responsible for the output of the entire group and will make sure that all other employees fulfill their individual roles, responsibilities and assignments.

The coordinator assures that all employees' efforts are focused and organized toward the accomplishment of the group's goal. Individuals in this role ensure there is no duplication of efforts and that the group is maximizing their performance and output.

The communicator is responsible for assuring that communication among all group members is maximized. They act as the primary coordinator of all group communications and reporting. One of the main functions is to halt any negative influences on the group's communication effectiveness.

The monitor watches the progress of the group and ensures that all work is performed on schedule and that all tasks and milestones are reached in determined time frames.

The group evaluator is responsible for seeing that all tasks and assignments within the group meet the performance standards agreed to by all members.

Other roles can be established and assigned to fulfill the varying needs of a group project.

Assigning Roles

When assigning roles, leaders must be able to assess and blend the strengths of individual employees. The purpose is to balance the efforts of the group, ensuring that all members are working together smoothly. No individual employee should overpower the combined efforts of the entire group.

Assigning specific roles to individuals is accomplished by assessing each employee's abilities and capabilities. It is done through addressing these following issues:

- What needs to be done?
- Which employees are available?
- Which employees are most capable?
- Who is willing?
- Who will get things done?

When leaders address these issues, they are able to identify the best individual match for a given role.

Leaders understand that initial efforts to assign roles and establish working groups can create problems and challenges. These occur most often when employees have not worked in this type of environment before. While it typically takes time and patience to resolve problems related to role assignments, the more a group collaborates on various project aspects, the more its harmony and productivity will improve.

POINTS TO PONDER — SOMETHING TO THINK ABOUT

1. Have you attempted to organize your employees into workgroups? What success have you had?
2. Have you developed roles for employees to fill within your workgroups? What were the results?

TRAINING ACTIVITY — APPLICATION & ACTION PLAN

1. Evaluate your employees for workgroup roles by asking the following questions:
    - What needs to be done?
    - Which employees are available?
    - Which employees are most capable?
    - Who is willing?
    - Who will be able to get things done?
2. Organize a working group by examining the following roles to determine

if they are adequate to meet your needs. Modify roles or add to them as needed to meet your specific requirements.

- Group Leader
- Coordinator
- Monitor
- Communicator
- Evaluator

3. Begin to assign specific roles on paper until you feel you have created a well-blended workgroup.

About the Author

Timothy F. Bednarz, Ph.D. is CEO of the American Management Development Group, Inc. For over 20 years he has researched, designed and authored hundreds of learning and development programs used by Fortune 1000 companies.

He is also the author of *Great! What Makes Leaders Great. What They Did, How They Did It and What You Can Learn from It* (2011).

Speaking Availability

Timothy F. Bednarz, Ph.D. is available for speaking engagements for your next meeting or association event. He can be contacted at 800-654-4935 or by e-mail at timothy.bednarz@majorium.com.

Bulk Sales

Bulk sales of this book or any other titles available from Majorium Business Press. Inquiries can be directed to sales@majorium.com, or by phone at 800-6654-4935.

Quick Order Form

Fax orders: 715-342-1118. Send this form.

Telephone orders: Call 800-654-4935 toll-free. Have your credit card ready.

Email orders: sales@majorium.com

Postal orders: Majorium Business Press, 2025 Main Street, Stevens Point, WI 54481, USA.

Please send the following books:

____

____

____

____

Please send more FREE information on:

❑Catalog ❑Speaking/Seminars ❑Mailing Lists ❑Consulting

Name: ____

Address: ____

City: ______________________ State: _____ Zip: __________

Telephone: ____

Email address: ____

Sales tax: Please add 5.5% for products shipped to Wisconsin addresses.

Shipping by air:

United States: $4.00 for first book and $2.00 for each additional product.

International: $9.00 for first book; $5.00 for each additional product (estimate).

Made in the USA
Monee, IL
04 November 2026

67377582R00031

Made in the USA
Monee, IL
04 November 2026

67377582R00031